A Beautiful

Disaster

By: Jason Buckley

A Beautiful

Disaster

By: Jason Buckley

This Book is Dedicated to the Best Thing that has ever come into my Life and the Best Thing in this World in my Eyes. MonkeyDOO, Monkey Bunkey, Ayden, AydenDoo. (The List of Names Could go On and On.) Daddy just Loves you So Much! I will never be able to tell you Enough in One Lifetime just how Much you mean to Me and How Much I just Love your Life. You are a True gift from GOD! There will never be enough days in my life with you and I will always love you with all my Heart. As we Both grow older, I know that we will grow closer! I can remember like it was yesterday when you grabbed daddy's finger for the first time. You gave me a look like you knew who I was and I have loved you ever since the beginning of your little life inside your mommy's belly. I Love you Soooooo Much.

This is one of the many things I will leave you with...But never forget how much you mean to me and even when you can't see me, I am always there with you; for you are a part of me. You will Always Be the Cutest Most Beautifulest Child I have Ever Laid Eyes On.

You are My Reason to Love, Smile and Believe that I had a chance to get this Book actually Completed... I love you so much
Ayden William Buckley

Xoxoxoxoxo

Love always and forever

Daddy!

To My Big Brother Adam and My Little Sister Jenny, I know life wasn't the easiest for us. Actually it was pretty fucking messed up and that's me trying to sugarcoat it. We all had it pretty rough but No matter the distance or Time apart; A bond like the one the three of us share can never be Broken. No matter how Broken things got; They could Never Break us! Life is Short and I know we Don't See much of each other But just know that I love you two like No Other!! We are Blood, We are Family. The Bond we share will Last Forever.

Adam, I will always look up to you No Matter What! You taught me to be Strong, you taught me how to be a Man, You taught me to Love myself for who I am; for those reasons and so many more I will Always Love You!!!! <3 <3 <3 <3

Jen, Jenny, My Little Baby Sister!!! I can never get over how old we all are getting!!! If anything makes me realize my age it's me realizing My baby sister just turned 33 Yesterday!! I can't wrap my head around it.. where have all the years Gone? I Love You more than you will ever know! I have and always will be proud to be one of your Big Brothers!! You Will Forever and Always be My Little Baby Sister!! No matter how old you get, you will Always be my Little Sister!!! I Love You so Fucking Much!!!

To My Mother And Father, Thank-You For Everything, If it weren't for you guys, I would not have been able to become a father myself to the Best thing in this World. Love you guys. xoxox

To Trish, One of the Greatest women I know and Also the Mother to my Son, I just want to take a second and Thank you for Everything! Thank you for showing me what it's like to be Loved by a Great Woman. Most importantly Thank you for Always Being There and Loving our Son. You are Truly an amazing Mother And I'm so proud of the Mother Ayden has allowed you to Become. We share something absolutely truly amazing. I will Never be able to Thank You Enough for our Son. You Gave me the Best Thing in this world and for that I will always Love You!! I Love Him so much and am Forever Grateful for Him. Thanks Again for Being the Best Mom you can be for Ayden!!

Xoxoxooxox

To everyone else that has come into my life at some point and either are still part of my life or not, I just want to thank you cause either big or small I have learned from you all. I have been blessed to meet a lot of great people in my life that I hold very close to my Heart. Just know when I tell you I love you, I truly Do. Life is one crazy ride and I want to thank each and everyone that has been along for the Trip. MUCH LOVE!!!

And Last But not Least! YOU! YES, YOU!! Thank you for giving this Book the shot it deserves. Thank you from the Bottom of My Heart!!! Now Sit Back, Buckle up and Enjoy Your Poetic Journey with Me!!! Thanks Again! Love You All!

Xoxoxoxox

Authors Note

I will Try to Keep this Nice and Short! I was Born in St. Stephens, New Brunswick Back in '83. Grew up in a Broken family, Spent the School years with my father in New Brunswick, And Christmas/Summer Holidays with my Mother in Kingston, Ontario! They Gave Me The Best life they knew how to; That's how I have come to terms with Everything that has happened throughout my life while living under their "care"! At 25, I Became a father to the Most Beautifulest Baby Boy in the whole world Named MonkeyDoo, Named by the nurse who Helped bring him into this world. It wasn't for a few days Till he later got his Name Ayden!! Mommy and Daddy Couldn't agree on a name. He has been My whole world since Day One!! All I knew was I was going to give him a better life than what I had had!

Moving Ten years ahead now I am still trying to give him the best life possible! He has and will always be my whole Heart and World!! We are Now living in Toronto with a Beautiful Baby Boy Frenchton Named Winston!! (Half Boston Terrier and Half French BullDog). I Have Also embarked on a New Relationship All While Finishing Up this Book that has been in the works long before Ayden came into My life!! There's Nothing Better Than the Love From your Son!! And Nothing Beats Puppy Kisses too!! I love you Ayden And Winston!!! <3 <3 <3 <3 I love you Mr..

Index

A Beautiful Disaster

By: Jason Buckley

Family

Families! They Are All Different in their own ways. Back in the day There was just your Traditional Families with your Mother and Father and their Children. Today in the world we live in its completely different. Some Families Have Two Fathers or Two Mothers, Plus added Step-parents. Some Children are being adopted out or raised by someone else in the family. No Family is Perfect, But Perfect in their Own Way. Well At least I'd like to think that about every Family Other than the one I came from.

I still try to find some kind of "Perfection" From the Family I was Brought in to, But the More I look, The more I search; I just realize how fucking broken that family was and continues to be. Siblings From Different men, All with a last name that Doesn't belong to them. Broken Dishes, Broken Down Dreams. Siblings Given away like Someone's Unwanted Trash. I was The First to go. I Always Dreamt Of what it would be like to be truly loved by a parent, It Was Always Just a Dream. Still to This day I often find myself still wondering what my life would have turned out like if I had had Loving parents Who Truly gave a Shit! All I knew back than Was if I Ever Brought a life into this Crazy World, Id make sure he never feels the way I do. He will Never Have To Wonder What its like to be Loved By a Parent. He Will Know Love! I Was Gonna Do Things Differently; I was Going to do Things Right!

All I know now is that My son will never Have to question if he is loved By his Father or Mother. He is Our World. He Has Been The light of our lives Since the day he entered this World. His Mother is One of the Most caring and loving mothers I know. I am Forever Grateful for all she does for My Baby Boy! I know he will never have to wonder what its like to Have a great mom, He has one of the Best! He will never Have to Wonder How His Old Man feels about him. He is my Whole World! He is The Reason I Smile, The Reason To Live! He knows I Love Him To The Moon And Back! I Love you MonkeyDOO! You Are My Family! You are My Everything! Lil Toes, Lil Nose; How I love it ALL!

<3 <3 <3 <3

The Moment I First Met You

From the moment I first met you,

I knew I'd love you forever!

So small yet so perfect,

Not even an hour old

And my hearts already been captured.

From the moment I first saw you,

I knew I was never letting go.

My little boy!

My Whole world!

You are My Everything!

From the moment I first met you,

I knew I found love!

You are My boy!

I am your Dad!

From the moment I first saw you,

I knew I'd Love You Forever!

9 Weeks

Young one don't fear,

For I will always be near.

I will hold you close

And love you the most.

A gift from god

Is what you are.

You are so perfect,

You are so great!

I am so excited,

That I just can't wait!

To hold you!

To love you!

Daddy just loves you so much!

Time won't go any faster

And I am counting down the days,

Till I get to hold you in my arms!

MonkeyDOO

Welcome to this Big Crazy World.

You may be scared and unaware

Of the World around you.

Never Fear MonkeyDOO,

For Mommy and Daddy will always be with you.

You are our little Monkey,

Our little Bundle of Joy!

You are so perfect, Only minutes old!

The world Changed, The Moment you arrived.

I Never knew true love,

till the moment I met you.

MonkeyDOO, Oh How I love you!

You are my little man, My New Best Friend!

Welcome to this Big Crazy World.

Daddy has your Back MonkeyDOO,

Always and Forever!

<u>Just Like Me</u>

There are days

You Drive Me Crazy,

There are days

You make me scream!

Every Day I love you more and more,

There's Never A Day that I Don't.

When you are not with me,

My World Isn't the Same.

We Are ONE of a Kinds

But Exactly the Same!

You are me; I am You!

On The Days You Drive Me Crazy

Or The Days you make me scream;

I Have to take the time

To Remind Myself that You're

Just Like Me!

Forever My BABY

No Matter

How Old You Get,

You Will Always Be

Forever My Baby.

You will Always Have Me

In The Palm of your Hands.

You Have Daddy

Wrapped Around your

Little Fingers.

Forever My heart,

Forever My Love,

Forever yours, Forever Mine.

Forever your Friend,

Forever Your Pal.

No Matter How old you are

Forever My Baby You'll Be. <3<3<3

LIL TOES

LiL Toes, LiL Nose

How I love it All!

So Beautiful, So Small

You're The Cutest Of Them All.

LiL Toes, LiL Nose

How I Love It All!

So Perfect, So Real

OMG, You're Such a BIG Deal!

LiL Toes, LiL Nose

How I love it All!

I Am Yours and You Are Mine,

You are Daddies One of A Kind.

LiL Toes, LiL Nose

LiL Toes, LiL Nose

Oh How I love you

Most of All!

Little Man of Mine

Little Man of Mine,

Oh how you shine.

Your Bright Smile

Could light up the darkest of Nights.

Your Beautiful Eyes

Are the Best I've Ever Seen.

You Are Perfect In Every Way!

Little Man of Mine,

You Are Defiantly One of A Kind;

No ones Just Like You.

Little Man of Mine

I Love You To The Moon and Back,

Always and Forever!

Daddy Is So Lucky To Call You Mine,

Little Man of Mine.

I Love You!

Ayden

Although you are my son I believe this to be true,

You're Simply Amazing; Truly A Gift from Above.

I Love You like No Other.

You Are Perfect, You are Great.

There's Nothing You Can't Do.

Don't Stop Trying, Never Give up.

Days will be Long And Some Nights Longer,

Keep Your Head Held High

And Always Shoot for the Stars.

Everyone Is Different,

No One is The Same, You are One of a Kind

Show The world what you have to Offer.

No Matter Where You go in life

Or whatever you may do

Daddy will always Be by your Side.

5

I can't Believe your 5!

Where has the time gone?

No More diapers, No More bottles!

Oh how I miss them both!

No more 3am feedings

Or cradling you in my arms.

You've Grown so much.

No Matter how old you get

Or how tall you become,

You will always be my Little Boy!

Kindergarten This year,

Boy Are you ever Smart.

I just know You're Gonna change this world!

I can't Believe Your 5, You're a little man now

But One thing will never change!

You will Always Be my Baby!

Dad

Thanks for always being there,

and never giving up.

You sheltered me from the cold,

When she no longer cared.

You gave me lots of love, when no one else would.

You gave everything you had, and so much more.

As long as I live, you will always be my daddy,

I love you more than life itself.

We are moving away from each other,

And life will never be the same!

For the longest time, we were inseparable.

As I write this, I cry!

I cry for the greatest times we had;

Camping, fishing and biking.

Not only were you a great dad,

You were always my Best friend!

Back into my Heart

I'm not sure how you do it,

But you do it every time.

We get in to a fight

You say very hurtful words, I cry!

Then I begin to hate you,

For all the times you broke This heart of mine

But time, and time again;

There you'll be just when I need someone the most.

I let you back into my heart

Hoping it would be the last time you'd leave;

Knowing it probably won't be.

You must stop this before it's too late.

Man, one of these times

I'm not going to open that door

And let you

Back in to this heart of mine.

Fatherhood

Suddenly awakened at 2 in the morning

From the cries of my son.

I rush into his room

Knowing he wants only the arms Of his loving father.

I place my pride and joy in my arms

And kiss him, and say I love yous.

The joy of holding him Brings a tear to my eye.

Knowing he's a part of me Puts a smile on my face.

Fatherhood will be ever lasting,

I will be a great dad   And a best friend.

For I know what's it like to be loved

By the best father in the world.

For every scrape & cut,

Look to your side And that's where I'll be

With Band-Aids & love.

I'll love you always; And the best father I will be!

Turn to Me

When you're lost

Turn to me,

I'll show you the right way

So you'll never be lost again.

When you're scared Turn to me,

I'll take your fears away.

When you're sad

Turn to me.

I'll tell you a hundred jokes,

Just to keep you smiling.

For anything & everything

Turn to me, I'll always be Here.

24/7/365 Days A Year.

Till the End of Time.

'Cuz I love you

Please remember to

Turn to me.

<u>Dear little One</u>

Dear little one

This is a promise to you,

That I'll always love you

And I won't ever give up.

Even when times get hard

I'll look into your eyes

And know things will get better.

I will never hurt you and always protect you,

Throughout your life

I'll always have your back

Call me day or night

And by your side I'll be.

I'll be there for You forever.

Dear little one

This is a promise to you,

That I'll always love you!

Time Lost

It's sad to think

Of all the years that have passed

Since I have seen you last.

Its sad to think that you

haven't held your grandson,

Changed a dirty diaper,

dried a falling tear.

Haven't told him a scary story or a funny joke!

Year after Year!

Moments that could have been,

memories that will never be!

Time never stopping!

Once a little bundle of joy,

now a little man.

So many holidays come and go

with out You Here.

Times you can never get back,

Memories that will never be made!

It's sad to think of the years that have past

Since I last seen you, dad.

You're so close, Yet worlds away!

It's sad to think about it,

So I try my hardest not too!

Happy Mother's Day

Today is your day

And I'd like to say,

Happy Mother's Day to you!

Thank you for all that you do,

Big or small you're there for them all.

We share a bond that will forever be!

You gave me a son.

One much more beautiful

Than the one in the sky

And became a beautiful mother.

You are his mommy,

But most of all, you're His Best Friend!

You are the Best Mother in the whole world,

And he loves you to no end.

Today is your day, And I'd like to say

Happy Mother's Day to you!

Brothers for Life

Forever My Big Brother You Will Be,

Life Wasn't Always the Best for You & Me

But We Made The Best Out of it.

We Might Not Have Always Seen Eye To Eye,

I Am Just As Hard Headed As You.

Even When You Were Right,

Even When You Were Wrong

I Still Looked Up To You.

You Will Always Be My Big Brother

Ill Always Look Up To You.

A Bond Like Ours Can Never Be Broken,

Blood Is Thicker Than Water.

Brothers For Life Is What We Are,

I Have Your Back

Yesterday, Today and Tomorrow.

Blood Is Thicker Than Water,

Brothers For Life is What We Are.

Inspiration

Inspiration can come from anything around you. I find my inspiration in the eyes of my beautiful son, From Puppy Kisses From Winston, In the arms of my loving Man And The Amazing People I work with (oh, Shane) And The Whole World Around Me! Everyday people just like you And I are being inspired by the people that are entwined in our Everyday lives. One Small moment in time can change the rest of your life Forever. I Hope these next few poems leave you with the Sense that you are a strong, one of a kind person whose dreams can come true; There is no one standing in the way But you! Also Remember that there is still good in the world and that it's not all about Hate and War. People Today need to keep the faith in Others and see the good in people before Noticing the Bad. Far too often we are judging the Book by its cover and missing out on truly knowing some very special people that walk in and out of our Lives Everyday. Every One of us Are Truly something special. We must find a common ground for man-kind to survive. If Everyone took a Little extra time From their BUSY lives to Be a Better person to first Themselves and secondly to the people around Them then the world would be a better place. It all starts with the person Holding this Book (YES! I'm Talking to you!) And a Little LOVE.

Xoxoxoxox

Go the Distance

Small Town Boy,

Living In The Big City.

Big City, Bigger Dreams.

The Sky Is The Limit,

Let's See How Far He Can Go.

Nothing Will Stop Him

Nothing will Get In The Way.

Small Town Boy

With Big Time Dreams.

Only One Life, Only One Shot.

Small Town Boy

Living In This Big World,

Let's See How Far I Can Go.

Nothing Will Get In My Way,

Nothing will Stop Me.

This Small Town Boy

Will Go The Distance.

Small Town

Who Would Have Thought
I'd Find Myself
In The Small Town Of Seagrave.
I Found More Than Just Myself.
I Found True Love,
I Found Family;
I Found Everything I was Missing.
Small Town,
Big Hearts.
I Found Myself
When I Found Seagrave.
I Found Family,
I Found Love.
This Small Town
Has Found its Spot in My Heart
And I Found Myself
In This Small Town!

Everybody

We Are All The Same,

As Much As You Don't Think So.

Whether Your Black or White, Yellow or Brown.

Whether Your Gay/Straight/ Bi /Trans.....

We Are All The Same,

As Much As You Don't Think So.

We All Have Fears, We All Get Scared.

We All Get Lonely, We All Want To Be Loved.

We Are All The Same,

As Much As You Don't Think So.

We All Have Hopes And Dreams..

We All Bleed When We get Cut; Cry, When We Get Hurt.

Everybody Deserves To Be Happy, To Be Loved.

Everybody Is Worth it!

Everybody!

We Are All The Same,

As Much As You Don't Think So.

But....

We ARE!

I'm Sorry

Saying Sorry Is Something I rarely do,

But It's Something I gotta Say to you!

I've Treated you like Shit,

Made you feel like you didn't matter.

No matter how strong you tried to be,

I always Found a way in

To break any piece of Hope you had left.

It was always so easy to break you down,

You were Already So Broken!

I would Kick you, when You were Down.

I'd cut You, Just to watch you Bleed.

There was No Safe Ground, No Hiding Spot!

You could never run away from me.

For I am you and you are me.

Saying Sorry, Is Something I rarely Do

But after seeing you in the mirror Today

I know its Something I have to do.

I Have found the courage to say,

I am Sorry for treating you that way.

I have found The Strength to Love you

Even on your worst of days.

You R Beautiful, I am Beautiful!

And I am Sorry!

Don't stop Believing

Don't stop believing,

In the person that you want to be.

GOD didn't make a mistake

When he planted you as a seed.

Don't stop believing,

In the places that you want to see.

You have two feet and a heart beat,

Life is a journey; keep pushing forward, and never look back.

Don't stop believing,

In the song that plays in your soul.

Listen with your heart

And dance the night away.

Don't stop believing,

In all that is good.

There is always a rainbow

After every storm.

Don't stop believing,

That you'll get where you want to be.

Enjoy life at your own pace, it isn't a race.

Don't stop believing,

In the person you want to be.

There is Only One You,

Let your colours shine!

One Life

We're Here For A Short Time,

Not A Long Time.

So Kick Up Some Dirt,

Get Some Mud On Your Boots.

Laugh Till Your Belly Hurts.

Dance As If,

No One Is Watching.

Sing As if,

The Whole World Can Hear You.

Love With All Your Heart And Soul.

Climb That Mountain,

Swim That Ocean.

Be All You Can Be.

You Are The Only You,

That Will Ever Be.

We're Here For A Short Time,

Not A Long Time.

Make All Your Dreams Come True,

Leave This Place With No regrets.

You Got One Life, Don't Waste It;

Make The Most Out Of It!

We're Here For A Short Time,

Not A Long Time.

So Kick Up Some Dirt,

Get Some Mud On Your Boots.

Thankful

When we come into this world

We are given our first breath of air;

Which we are Thankful for.

As we grow,

We are blessed with many things,

Which we can not give enough Thanks for.

Some days are Tough,

Some nights are Long.

Life can be Hard.

But... Be Thankful for what you Have.

Life is short! <<<Live it Up>>>>

Life! Laugh! Love!

When we leave this world,

We are given our last breath.

Which we are Thankful for!

I gave my Life

Being shot in the head,

Wishing I was home in bed.

Wondering how much blood

I have actually bled.

Trying to stand to my feet,

I take a few steps, and then take a seat.

Wishing I could defend my people,

but I'm beat. Thinking of the family I could have had,

The thought of it makes me feel sad.

Knowing that my son would have been a great lad.

Fighting to stay alive,

I close my eyes and think of the fight I put up.

Knowing that I made a lot of people proud of me.

Knowing I'm about to die, I pray!

I pray to god, for a tomorrow that is not gray.

I know that day is about to come our way.

Knowing I'll go to heaven

For the love of my people, I just want them to know that

I gave my life to be a veteran.

Anything is Possible

Everyday seems different,

New emotions fill this heart of mine.

Some of them scare me

And others worry me.

Others fill me with hope and promise!

My world is changing before my eyes

And I feel as though I'm not moving fast enough.

Soon I'll be left behind in the dust of others.

I'm dying inside with every passing day.

I want answer to all the questions I have.

I know that's impossible!

I want to know the meaning of life

Or the reason I was put on this earth.

So as I sit here and think things through,

All the people I love are leaving me behind.

I stand up and a make a decision.

I'm going to live life to the fullest

And deal with what life gives me.

Life is too short,

To sit and think!

You must take a stand

And live out your dreams;

For anything is possible!

Every Morning

Every morning,

I Thank God

For another Day with You.

To watch you as you sleep

Is a blessing in It self.

Every Night,

I Thank God

For another night with you.

With you in my arms

There's No places I'd rather Be.

I Thank the Big Guy all the Time;

For making you Mine.

He Has a Greater plan for Us

just You wait and see.

A plan in which we become Three.

A Baby Boy is what it will Be.

A Bundle of joy, A Gift of Life.

A Blessing from up Above.

Every Morning

And

Every Night

I give Thanks to the Big Guy.

For Bringing you Two into My Life.

So as this poem comes to an end, I Thank God

For another Night with You.

You are not Alone

If you ever feel like you are alone in this big world,

Chances are you're probably not.

If you are the one that cry themselves to sleep,

You are not alone.

If you ever think about suicide,

You are not alone.

If your heart has been broken more than once,

Sorry pal, But you are still not alone.

Open your heart and talk to people.

Soon you will see that people are going through

The same as you and I.

Soon You will realize that

You are not alone.

Everyone's a Critic

You can kick me down

But don't expect me to remain on the ground.

For I will rise again,

I've worked to hard to be brought back down.

Don't waste your breath,

I don't need your acceptance.

The light in my eyes will always be

brighter than the sun in the sky.

Criticism will not put out this flame.

Poetry is a part of me; A part of my Life.

Read it and enjoy it, Read it and criticize it.

Which ever you choose to do,

I will always write.

Be who you are, Do what you do

Because some will Love

And Some will Hate.

Either way they will Have something to Say!

Beautiful Morning

A beautiful morning

Is what this is.

As I sit peacefully

On my front step,

I watch and listen

To the sounds of this Big Crazy World.

The Birds fly High, The ants walk low.

I sit in amazement,

Watching the rising sun

Peaking through the clouds;

Puts a warm loving feeling in my heart.

I sit for a little longer And than go inside

To hear the cries from my newborn son.

I wish to myself That every morning

Could be this beautiful.

As I pick my little buddle of joy up, I soon realize

When I hold you in my arms, I hold the world;

Because you are the world to me,

You are what makes life so beautiful.

Maybe Tomorrow

Sitting in class wishing I could tell you how I feel.

I know that what I feel is real.

I stop in the hall to look into your eyes,

Do you even know I'm alive?

Wanting so bad to hold you tight,

Wishing I could tell you that it might be right.

Hearing your laugh sends shivers down my spine,

Being without you makes me feel like

I'm living a lie.

So until I have the nerve to tell you, how I feel;

I'll sit back and stare, and wonder if your even real

Or maybe just a figment of my imagination.

Maybe tomorrow I'll tell you how I feel.

Maybe tomorrow!

Big Enough

The World Is Big Enough

For You!

The World Is Big Enough

For Me!

The World Is Big Enough

For Her!

The World Is Big Enough

For Him!

The World Is Big Enough

For Us All!

Lets Play

Instead of Fighting.

Lets Love

Instead of Hating.

The World Is Big Enough For Everyone,

So Why Can't We Just Get Along!

Love

LOVE! Such a small word, but yet it's the thing that would change the world for the Better. Love is really all we need. Poetry was started on the Basis of love; you can't have poetry without speaking about Love. It would be like a song without words, a sea without fish. You just couldn't do it. Poetry is your Hearts way to let your feelings out. There's nothing better than letting your heart do the talking. Besides what would us men give to that special someone in their lives? It's a last minute gift which is sure to please for people who have a tendency to forget special occasions, not to mention that it means a lot considering it's from the heart. I have had my share of moments of True Love and also True Lust. A lot of people these days get the two Twisted...LOL... Love can either Make you or Break you. They say that everyone has their soul-mate; When you find yours, hold on tight and don't let go. You only Live once, so may you have a life full of love. I Hope you enjoy my outlook on the power of Love! The Good, The Bad, The Crazy and The Beautiful...

Since Starting this Poetic Journey, I Have had The chance to feel all those feelings! I Had The chance to fully feel like Someone's Prince, Someone's Love of their life, Someone's Petite Chou! I got to feel the strongest of love, the purest of lust. I was Blessed to feel the butterflies and all those moments that seem to be to good to be true that you question if your awake or Dreaming. I Thought I had found forever, My soul-mate and all that. Truth of the matter is Love is not what you always think it is. It also doesn't Always turn out the way you think it will. I Have had the chance to feel the Bad, The Shitty, The Sleepless nights thinking you couldn't go on another day. Life is Crazy, You Never know what tomorrow will Bring. I don't know if there is that person out there for me. I know one thing for sure; I Will always continue to love with all my Heart. Nothing or No one can Change that. Most importantly Always Love Your-Self; If you Don't Love Your-Self, How in The Hell can you Love Any One Else. As This Book is Being Finally completed, I Have embarked on a New Relationship. One In which is Different from all The rest, Two Hearts on a cold Street! I'm Not sure if it will last forever, I'm not sure if Tomorrow He will wake up and realize I'm not the one for him. I'm not sure of anything when it comes to this Crazy thing called Love anymore. I'm Not Being A Hater, I'm Just Saying Love is a Crazy Thing. I Have Loved, Been Loved. I Have Also Been on the Flip side of Things. I Have let this Heart of mine take me on some Crazy Journeys so far in my life.

As I finish up this chapter on my mac book in my condo in Toronto; With My New Man Snoring away on the sofa, I have to just sit here and smile. You really Never know where you will end up in this life. Don't Stop living, Don't Stop loving. You Only LIVE ONCE; LOVE WITH ALL YOUR HEART. I Have to take it all in for what it is now! It may not last forever But The Here and now is looking And Feeling Great! I Have Fallen in Love All Over Again. I am Now Someone's Lobster! Never Give up on LOVE! You Are Meant To Love, You Are Meant To Be Loved! With That Being said I'm Going to get me some snuggles In before He wakes up!   ENJOY!

XOXOXOX!

Hello There

Hello There,

Is How This All Started.

One Lonely Night

While I Sat At Home

Over Shitty Wi-Fi.

We Made A Connection

Through Text And Calls;

The Connection Only Got Stronger.

Where We Will Go,

No One Knows.

It All Started With

Hello There.

If We Can Stay Connected

Than We Will Never Have To Say

Good-Bye!

Dream

Am I Awake

Or Am I Dreaming?

Is This Real

Or Just All In My Head?

Am I Awake

Or Am I Just Dreaming?

Seems Too Good To Be True.

I Must Be Dreaming;

If I Am Dreaming

I Never Want To Wake.

Am I Awake

Or Am I Just Dreaming?

Only Time Will Tell,

I'm Hoping That Your Real

And Not Just In My Head.

Am I Awake

Or Am I Just Dreaming?

'Cuz You're a Dream To Me.

This is Crazy

This Is Crazy,

This Is Nuts.

Where Did You Come From,

Where Have You Been?

None Of That Matters,

As Long As You're here With Me.

This Is Crazy,

This Is Nuts.

You have Me Falling,

You Have Me Floating.

You Have Me Feeling Things

I've Never Felt Before.

This Is Crazy,

This Is Nuts.

Am I Loosing My Mind

Or Could You Be The One

I've Been Dreaming of!

Same Page

Two Peas In A Pod

Are What We Are.

You Get Me

Like I Get You.

Two Hearts, Beating To The Same Song.

We Found Ourselves

When We Found Each Other.

We Are A Perfect Match.

It's Awesome To Be

On The Same Page, For Every Thing.

You Were Made For Me

Like I Was Made For You.

Two Hearts,

One Page,

One Love.

I Love You!

It was always You

It Didn't Work With Him
Because It Wasn't Meant Too.
It Was Always You.
I Just Hadn't Met You Yet.
Timing Is Everything,
Two Hearts On A Cold Street.
Looking For Each Other,
Finally Together;
Never To Be Alone Again.
I Got You, You Got Me.
We Found Love, We Found Forever
When We Found Each Other.
It Didn't Work out With him
Because It Wasn't Supposed Too.
It Was Always You,
I Was Meant For You
NO ONE ELSE!

What's Wrong With You

What's Wrong With You,

'Because I Can't Find Anything.

Your Perfect In Every Way.

Your Fucking Amazing,

You Amaze Me Every Day.

What Is Wrong With You,

No One Is This Perfect.

I Look & Look

And Still Come Up Empty Handed.

Not Only Are You Perfect,

You're Perfect For Me.

I'm Not Sure If This Is Fate

But Damm Boy, You Were Worth The Wait.

I Can't Find Anything Wrong With You,

Your Perfect In Every Way.

Most Importantly

Your Perfect For Me.

What's Wrong With You

Nothing...

Your Perfect...I love you!

Not Over

Life is Not Over, Now That Your Gone.

Life Has Only Just Begun

Since You've Said Good-Bye.

Not Gonna Lie

Thought I Would Die.

This Hasn't Been Easy

Many Tears have Fallen.

Every Day

I Get A Little Stronger

Now That I know

Life Isn't Over, Since You've Said Good-Bye.

Everyday

I Get Stronger & Stronger.

I Thought I would Die

But The Day You Left

I Started Living.

Life's Not Over, Now That Your Gone

It Wasn't You

It Wasn't You,

It Wasn't Me,

It Was Us.

We Weren't Meant To Be.

A Forever is what We Wanted

But...

It Wasn't In The Stars 4 Us.

You Weren't Right Or Wrong

And Neither Was I.

A Love like Ours

Was Meant To Die.

It Wasn't you,

It Wasn't me,

We Weren't Meant To Be.

Can't Let Go!

Can't Let Go,

Even if I Tried.

Your Still in My Head

But No Longer in My Bed.

You'd Love Me Forever,

Is What You Said.

Can't Let You Go,

Even if I Tried.

Still Trying To Figure Out

How You Let Go Of ALL

Our Love,

Our Plans,

Our Dreams,

Our Forever!

I Will Love You Forever,

Miss You Always!

Can't Let Go,

Even if I Tried.

I Just Can't;

I'll Hold You Forever

And Ever!

Broken Down

Broken Down

On The Side

Of The Road.

Not Really How

I pictured This Night would Go.

Our First Date,

In a Car That won't Go.

A Spark in My Heart,

A New Love Had Started

That Night

In the Broken Down Charger.

Our First Kiss

Won't Ever Be Forgotten.

It Happened on our First Date

While We Were Broken Down

On The Side of the 401....

<u>Only One Key</u>

There's Only One Key,

To this Heart of Mine.

Only One Key that fits,

Only One Key to unlock

The Love, The Joy.

There's Only One Key To This Heart of Mine.

Only One Heart, That Belongs to that Key.

Together a Whole,

Apart Just Halfs.

There's Only One Key

To this Heart of Mine,

No Other Key Will Do.

You Have the Key

To This Heart of mine.

Together A Whole,

Apart Just Halfs.

Together Forever,

Forever as One.

Charger

It all started in the Charger,

The moment I opened

The passenger door.

I knew we'd be more than friends.

You gave me your hand

And made me weak in the knees.

I knew right than and there,

I never wanted you to let go.

My heart raced faster

Than that Dodge that night.

You made me a believer of

Love at first sight.

In the still of the night

With the moon just right,

Your lips met mine.

I could feel

The beating of your heart

Against my chest.

With just one kiss,

I knew that man

In the charger

Was going to be mine.

Fate was finally falling into place.

Man in the Photo

I had a Photo Sent to me,

Sexiest Man I have Ever seen!

Perfect in Every way.

Perfectly Tanned,

Perfectly Beautiful.

Man in uniform,

Sexy as can be.

Leaning against bathroom stall,

Lit smoke in mouth.

Smoking Hot, In All the right Spots.

Man of my Dreams,

Man of my world.

I may have lost that photo

But I have you in my arms now.

Man in the Photo,

Sexy as can Be, Now Belongs to Me.

<u>A walk to Remember</u>

A walk to remember,

Is what it was.

The First time we met,

The First time we kissed!

A walk to Remember,

Is what it was.

A Fond memory,

I'll always hold dear.

A walk to Remember,

Is what it was.

Who would have thought,

That I would Find some one like you!

What do you call This

Sitting here

Starring into your eyes,

Wishing I knew

How you felt

on the Inside.

So Quite,

So Beautiful,

So Perfect

In Every way!

Sitting here

Holding you close I ask,

What do you call this?

You Say....

It feels like a dream,

Too Good to be true!

Forever Yours

From the Moment I first saw you,

I knew right then

I never wanted to let go.

You are so sexy,

You are so fine.

One day if I am lucky

I will be able to call you Mine.

From the Moment

I kissed your soft lips,

I knew right then

I had fallen for you.

From the moment I met you

I knew right than,

we would be more than just friends.

Turns out.....

We will be lovers till the End.

YOU on THAT Dance Floor

Bright lights, Loud music;

Dancing to the beat.

With you on this dance floor

Is where I want to be.

Holding you, Touching you;

Moving to the beat.

Loving Every minute

With You on this dance floor.

There's No place I'd rather be.

Sweaty Bodies, Bare skin.

You are Just to fine,

Oh how I Love to call you Mine.

Party doesn't stop at 2am

Because you are mine,

I get to take you Home...

Every Time!

City Lights

City Lights

Holding you Tight,

Everything feels so right.

So perfect,

So True.

I'm so happy I found

Forever in you.

You are My World,

You are My Life.

When You are in My arms,

Nothing else matters.

Theses City Lights,

Holding you Tight;

Life couldn't Get any Better.

You're Even More BEAUTIFUL

You're even more Beautiful

Than the day before.

I fall in love with you Every time

Our eyes meet.

Late at Night

You're even more Beautiful,

Than the stars in the sky.

I only Hope to

Hold you for a Life-Time,

Like The Sky Holds the Moon.

You're Even more Beautiful,

When you Look into My Eyes

And Tell Me That

You Love Me.

Never Want to Wake

I Never want to wake

If this is just a Dream.

If you are not real

And all of this was a Dream

Than I want to sleep Forever,

Just to hold you in my arms.

A love like this is to good to be true.

So If this is not Real

Than let me be the last to know.

Never wake Me,

Let me sleep Forever;

Just so I can hold you tight.

I find it hard to believe

That this is not a Dream.

So if this is a Dream,

Please Never wake me

So I can hold you Forever.

Found You

I was lost,

Didn't know what was Up or Down.

I found Myself,

When I Found you.

In your arms,

I am no longer lost,

I am no longer scared.

In You I Found a Friend,

In You I Found a Lover.

I once was lost

But Now I am Found.

I Found Myself,

When I Found You.

Never Lost, Never Alone;

The Day I Found You

Is the day I Found ME.

Forbidden Love

Forbidden Love,

Is what they Call Us.

Let them talk, let them stare.

What Do they know, Why should they care.

Love is Love,

Even if its Two Men.

Forbidden Love

Is what they Call Us.

Let them talk,

Let them stare.

If this is wrong,

Than I don't Ever want to Be Right.

Forbidden Love

Is what they Call Us,

But They Don't Know

What it's like to be Loved by YOU.

The Pier

Our Very Own place In this Big World,

No one can take it away.

It's Mine, It's Yours, It's Ours.

Our Meeting place, If we ever lose our way.

The place we became one,

No one can take that away.

I am Yours, You are Mine; Together We Are Whole.

Everything's So Perfect,

The Stars, The moon;

The water crashing against the rocks.

There's Only One Man

That I want to

Hold Forever, Love Forever.

I wrote Our Names on the pier

Just to show the world

How much I LOVE YOU...

<u>My Vows</u>

My Vows Are Simply

But True.

I fell in love,

The moment I Met you.

You are My Rock, You are My Glue.

You are My apple to My pie,

You are The Sugar to My Coffee.

You Are My Everything.

Yesterday, Today, Tomorrow and Forever!

I will Love you like No Other

And Even When Our Time Is up

On This Little Planet

We Call Earth,

Our Journey Doesn't End

Cause When I say Forever;

Our Forever Has No End!

Till My last Breath

Till My Last breath

I want you by my side.

I want to feel your love

All around me

Till My Last Day on Earth.

You Make my heart skip a beat

When your lips touch mine.

My body Fills with Butterflies

With the thought of you.

Till my Last Breath,

You will be mine,

I will be yours.

I will Love You Then

Like I Love You Now

With Every Beat of My HEART......

In My Eyes

In my eyes,

You can find Forever!

So what are you waiting for?

In my eyes,

You can find the truth!

My Love is real,

My Love is pure!

Just give me the Chance

To prove my Love to you.

Give me your Hand,

Ill Never let you Down.

Give me the Chance,

To Be your Man.

In My eyes,

you can find Forever!

So what are you waiting for?

Silent Nights

A silent night,

A moon held high.

Thoughts of you,

Run through my mind.

A silent night,

A river runs deep.

Thoughts of you run through my Blood.

A silent night,

Millions of stars shinning Bright.

Thoughts of you,

Flow through my body.

On silent nights,

When I'm all alone.

Thoughts of you,

Linger in my heart.

Bottled Emotions

Bottled Emotions,

Kept inside!

Hope to revel them

Before I die.

If I die,

Before I do!

Place a rose on my grave

And know that I loved you!

Always have, Always will!

For the sun will rise in the morning

But by your side, I will not be!

For I have gone,

Gone from this world.

A love like ours will last a lifetime

And I would wait till the end of time

To hold you in my arms once again.

I Love You

Love is a great thing.

Take care of it and it will grow

Into something more magical

Than some have ever seen in their life.

If not, it will go down the drain

Like yesterdays garbage disposal.

So as I write this,

I'm losing the one I love

Because of my stupid broken heart!

How do I say I love you to them

When those three words

Are what caused my heart to break!

Maybe he is not like my ex!

Maybe he is the one!

Only one way to find out.

Let the past be the past.

Everything happens for a reason.

All I can say is

Fallow your heart; it might lead you the right way

Or it may lead to heartache.

Either way never miss the chance to say...

I LOVE YOU!!!

Love will find the Way

Looking in your eyes,

I feel the love you send to me.

I hear the words that you aren't able to speak.

Talking to you,

I feel the kindness in your heart,

I hear the softness in your voice.

Being friends with you,

Brings happiness and freedom to my life

And that's how I know somewhere down the road;

Love will find the way.

You found your way to my heart,

A place you can call home;

Where you will never be lonely again.

I am yours and you are mine.

Love will find the way

Because I am here to stay!

6 Roses

I gave you 6 roses And this is why.

The first rose

Is for the smile on your face.

A smile that could light up a night sky.

The second rose

Is for the light in your eyes.

For I know I'll find the truth there.

The third rose

Is for your strong hands.

The hands that pick me up when I'm down.

The forth rose

Is for your heart.

The heart that is pure of gold.

The fifth rose

Is for your soul.

It's always your goal to make people happy.

The last rose

Is for the love that we share.

A love that is more beautiful than these flowers.

If you were Here

If you were here,

I'd hold you forever

So you'd never leave my side.

If you were here,

I'd love you with all my heart

Praying that our love wouldn't fall apart.

If you were here,

I'd tell you a lot of jokes,

Just to see your beautiful smile

But you're not here.

So I'm left alone,

Only to wonder

What I'd do if you were here.

Forever and More

When your world seems cold,

I'll be there

With my hands to warm your heart.

For I am a friend, and forever

I'll be there! When ever you feel alone!

Call my name, because you should know

I'll be there!

I don't mind opening my heart to you.

For I know you'd never break it!

I can see us getting closer With every passing day.

Your friendship will stay with me

Forever and more!

For you are the one who opened my eyes

And let me see the real world.

You've made your mark in my heart

And that's where you'll stay.

I Wonder

I wonder!

Who's face you see when you close your eyes?

I wonder!

Whose kiss you need,

In the middle of the night

I wonder!

Who's the person who has your heart

And doesn't know it!

I wonder!

Could the person be me?

Would it ever be me? Could it ever be me?

I just wonder;

If I will ever have the chance to hold you tight?

Kiss you at night? Be the man to love you right.

I lay here staring up into the night sky

And just ponder.

No Words

There are no words to say,

How much I love you.

Those 3 words aren't enough,

To tell you all that I feel for you.

Even through our UP's and down's

There are still not enough words to tell you.

How much I need you, want you, and love you!

You have a special place in my heart,

Every time it beats; it beats for you.

So now I search for words

To express my love for you

But there are still not enough words.

To tell you how much I love you!

I can't help Myself

I can't help myself,

When the sound of your voice

Tells me you love me.

I can't help myself,

When your tempting lips Press against mine.

I can't help myself,

When you run your fingers through my hair

Whispering loving words in my ear.

I can't help myself,

When We lay in bed together

Holding me close to you.

Whatever you seem to do,

It has the same reaction.

Every time, No matter what!

I can't help myself! I want all of you,

All To Myself,

For the Rest of My Life!

Thoughts of Love

When I think of love,

I think of you.

Holding you, Touching you,

Loving you!

When I dream of love,

I dream about you,

Holding you,

Touching you,

Loving you!

So when I find you!

I know I'll be

Holding you,

Touching you,

Loving you!

The way I was when I had

Thoughts of love.

I'll try to Say

In this poem, I'll try to say

Just how much you mean to me.

How much I needed you!

You came into my life like a breath of fresh air

And mended my heart That once was broken.

You took me in your arms

And loved me with all that you are.

In the morning I awake before you,

Just to watch you sleep.

I love waking up beside you Because you are my man,

My love, My world; My Everything!

You now should know.

Just how much I care.

What I am trying to say is

I love you!

J'Taime Mon Gross Chou!!!

<u>I will never leave You</u>

Those words are hard to say sometimes

But as for me, these words are no lie.

My love for you will never Die.

I know that some day I will have to leave

But for this time, I would like to stay.

If I were to leave now, I don't think I would find my way

Walking down the road of life, with the love of my dreams.

Together and forever, me and you as a team.

Team Chou!

I will Never Leave you!

Because I Love you!

_I Do_

I Do!

Will be 2 words,

That will change my life.

I will only say them

To the person who has

My heart in the palm of their hands;

Knowing they will never break it.

I'll give them a ring as a sign of my love.

On the day I say I do,

A whole new life will start.

In the new life there will be much love and joy.

I do!

Funny how 2 small words

Can change your life forever!

So now all I can do is wait

Till the day I say.....I do!

No Warranty

I give my love to you,

At no cost.

Without a warranty.

Treat it well

And it will stay.

Mistreat it

And I'll take it back.

Giving it to you is hard,

Taking it back isn't!

Acknowledge it while it's there

Cause when it's gone!

You'll never get it back.

Dreaming

Laying in bed, thinking of you.

Wishing and praying,

That someday that we'll be together

Building a life of love!

Hoping to share my dreams with you,

Wishing I could find the right words

To tell you how I feel but for now

It's only in my head...

and I'm still in my bed.

alone!

Dreaming of you.

If walls could Talk

If walls could talk,

They would tell you

That I cry

From the bottom of my broken heart.

They would tell you,

You're all I think about,

You're all I dream about.

If walls could talk,

You would know how I feel

And how I wish you were here.

They would tell you

That you have my unconditional love.

If walls could talk they would tell you,

I love you!

Poem for You

I write this poem for you,

For when I look into your eyes

The only words that come out

Are I love you's.

I have so much to say to you,

When you are with me

Nothing else matters.

If I get you back; I'm never going to let go

People make mistakes.

And the biggest one I could ever make

Is to let you walk out of my life.

So as I write this poem for you;

The words still won't come out.

All I can seem to think about these days

Is how much I love you.

Hopefully when you read this

You'll realize just what you mean to me

Because I love you

And this poem is for you.

Loving' You

This is a promise to you,

I've change for the better

To keep you in my life.

I'll never make you cry again,

I'll hold you close during the storm.

I'll do anything to put a smile on your face.

I never want you to feel

Like you're wasting your life with me.

I want you to be proud to be mine.

I love you Baby And that's why I'm here.

To keep loving' you All through the 4 seasons

And the years to come.

I'll stay by your side.

This is a promise to you.

I've change for the better,

I've changed for the good.

One things for sure

I'll do what I can

To keep you in my life.

Never Change

As I sit up in bed

Watching you dream away.

I realize just how beautiful

You really are

And how lucky I am

To have you in my life.

I know we have had hard times

But through it all, it was worth it

To look in your eyes

And know how much you really care,

Is worth more to me.

I love you now, like I'll love you tomorrow

With all my heart and soul.

And it will Never Change.

Once Alone

When we touch,

My heart races.

When we kiss,

butterflies fill my soul.

You put the light in my eyes,

So please don't put it out.

Life without you, would be just wrong.

I need you, Cuz I love you.

I love you, Cuz you're beautiful.

Your smile, could light up the darkest room.

Baby, I love you now

Like I'll love you forever.

You've captured my heart

By just taking my hand

And walking me down the road

Where I once walked alone.

Changed Dreams

I once Dreamt

Of lying on a bed of roses,

But now I only Dream

Of lying in bed with you.

I once Dreamt

Of running away from everyone

But now I only Dream

Of running to you.

I once Dreamt

About dying and leaving this place for good

But now I only Dream

Of living with you for the rest of my life.

Dreams can change with just the right person.

Ten billion fish may be in that sea

But you're the only one for me.

Undying Love

A new day has come

And you're still the only one.

I never want to know a life

Without you by my side.

Seasons come

And seasons go

My love for you

Will always grow.

With tomorrow

A new day will come

And by my side

I hope you'll be.

As the days get warms

And the nights get cooler

I will love you more and more

As I did when we were younger.

We walk Together

We walk together as a team,

Our hearts will never part

Because we are meant to Be.

With our hands tight together

We can walk through life's challenges

With no sweat on our brow.

Life will go on

And my love for you will forever show.

As we grow older

And our hair turns grey.

We will walk together

Hand in hand

Our hearts will never part.

Because we are meant to be.

People say I'm Crazy

People say I'm Crazy

And you can believe it's true

But I started believing in miracles

The moment I saw you.
People say I'm Crazy

And you can believe it's true.

But I see forever

When looking into your eyes.

People say I'm Crazy

And you can believe it's true

But when I fall asleep

I only Dream of you.

People say I'm Crazy

And you can believe it's true

But I threw my love away

And gave up too soon.

People say I'm Crazy

And you can believe it's true

But until my dying day, I will always love you.

Lost Love

Scattered pictures On the floor!

Lost in Memories,

Searching for answers.

why did you leave,

why didn't you stay?

Rip, Snip, Tear!

Torn pictures all over the floor.

Ruined Dreams,

Lost Love!

It must be me!

I just don't get it.

Beautifully broken,

Too Damaged to be Loved.

Forever Alone!

Scattered pictures on the floor,

Lost in the Mess!

Sad Good-Byes

Life is what you make it! You can choose to have the Best Life in the world or the Shittiest one, In the end we all die. Before we die, we must do one of the hardest things in life; We must say goodbye to the ones we Love. It's the Hardest part of life. You Meet and come to Love all these People/Animals that you let into your World and into your Heart! One day they are just gone, never to be seen or heard from Again. You're left praying and wishing that there is a place called Heaven; where everyone will be together again. No one really knows for sure. Until that day comes; I will find myself remembering the ones that I have had to say Goodbye too, But also keeping my faith that one day I will see them Again. The Memories that you make with these people will Live On and On Forever in Our Hearts. So with all that Being said this chapter is all about saying SAD GOOD-BYES... To the Ones that I have Had to say those words to... You guys are still with me every step of the way and these are for you. Love you <3 <3<3

This Honestly is the Hardest chapter in the Book! During the writing process of this book, I had to say Good-Bye to someone that I never imagined saying those words too. The sadder Part is I wasn't around to fix anything or make it Better. I thought time would heal it all and did NOTHING! I messed up and Did nothing! I missed the chance to make it right, I missed the chance to tell her how much she really meant to me. She's Just gone, And I'll Never Have That Chance again! I love and Miss you so much Granny Buckley! You were one of a kind! You were everything a Grandmother could be and

More! You are the reason I Pray there's A Heaven; Just to See you Again! Don't Be silly like me and let time pass you by! We don't know how long we have here! Live with no Regrets! If You fucked up, Own it and fix it before you lose that chance to say you're sorry. Once That Chance is gone, Its gone! So With that Being said.......

I LOVE YOU GRANNY BUCKLEY! I AM SOOO SORRY FOR EVERYTHING! ONE DAY I'LL SEE YOU AGAIN.. I'LL MAKE IT ALL RIGHT! XOXOXOOX

Little Angel Of Mine

Little Angel of Mine,

I loved you since the Beginning,

Will Love You Always.

I'll Meet You in Heaven,

Where I'll hold You Forever.

I'll Never get Why You had to Leave,

I'll Always Picture what could have been.

Little Angel of Mine, I had to Say Goodbye

Before you learnt how to say Hello.

I Loved You Since Day One,

I'll Love You Forever.

Little Angel of Mine,

I'll See you on the Other side,

Where I'll Hold You Forever.

Little Ivy May, Mommy and Daddy Love You.

For Now and Always.

Little Angel of Mine,

We Will meet You in Heaven

And Be Together Forever.

<u>Nobody told Me</u>

Nobody Told Me,

That You had to go!

Nobody Told Me,

That You couldn't stay!

I never knew You left us

and went to the clouds above.

Nobody Told Me,

Your Time had come.

Nobody Told Me,

I would have Been There.

I never had the chance to say Goodbye.

Nobody Told Me,

Ignorant Fuckers!

Nobody Told Me

That you had to Go.

I would have Been There!

But....

Nobody Told Me!

Gone Too Soon

Lost down Memory lane,

Thoughts of you always linger.

The softness of your lips,

The scent of your body.

Gone way too soon

Forever Missed, Forever Loved.

Until We meet again,

I hold all our memories dear.

You were My First Love,

You were my True Love.

Gone Too Soon.

Lost Down memory lane

is Where I can often be found,

Just to see you again.

To hold you, To Kiss you, To Smell you.

I wish this wasn't real,

But you are gone. Gone too Soon

And I'm left with just memories,

Until I can Be with you again.

Colouring

We used to color together,

It was a once in a lifetime thing.

Now you are too far away,

For us to share our crayons.

I wish you were here

Because you have the missing crayon

That would make this world a prettier place.

You were only here for a short time

But in that time you showed us your magical smile.

A Smile That Could

Light up the darkest skies.

Spreading Bright colors where ever you went.

I can't wait to be with you again

For I know We'll colour the Heavens!

I love you Amanda!

Happy Birthday

Happy Birthday Rocky!

Although this is your last,

Nov. 24 will always be your day.

You'll always be a part of our family.

You'll leave your paw prints

In the hearts of the people you've touched.

We gave you everything

A cat could ever ask for.

We love you more than you'll ever know.

As your Birthday comes, Tears come to my eyes,

Knowing this will be your last.

Making it the best one you had,

Wishing you could stay but

Knowing your going to a better place.

Letting you go it going to be hard, but

I'll be strong for you.

Rocky you've made our life so much Happier.

Happy Birthday to you!

I love you Rocky!

Christmas without You

Thinking of Christmas.

Makes me think of you, Lying under our tree.

One happy Cat Getting into all the gifts.

You were meant to be there

For you were always a gift to us.

Christmas morning was fun,

You always got lost in the wrapping paper.

This Christmas will not be the same.

I won't see you under the tree,

Or under the wrapping paper

But I know where to find you

I just have to look inside This heart of mine.

For you'll always be there.

Christmas without you

Is going to be hard.

Living without you

Is going to be Harder.

Until we meet Again

Dear child,

I felt the pain with in my heart,

That cold winter day you left us.

We all know now that you are in a better place.

I just want you to know that your mom loves you dearly.

We all think about you day and night,

How we miss you so.

I'm sad to say,

That you'll never know how much we loved you.

I feel bad through my tears.

That you'll have no first words.

Words that could have changed our world.

No girl of your dreams, No prom night for you.

All of these things, you left undone.

For you are now gone, gone away.

You will always Be In our hearts,

Until we meet again.

Lost in Memories

Lost in memories of you.

Knowing that's all that will be,

When you leave us

To go into your endless sleep.

I know we'll meet again,

It's just we'll miss you dearly.

We had you since you were a kitty.

14 years have gone by Yet not a memory lost.

Not one will ever be forgotten.

As that day gets closer, I realize I have to let go

Of something I only started

To hold on to dearly.

Rocky, I love you, You'll always remain with me.

Lost in memories of you.

Knowing that's all that will be

When you leave us!

Never to make new ones.

Leaves me,

Lost in memories.

Our Hearts Were Not...

Your wings were ready,

Long before our hearts

were ready to say good-bye.

We would have always wanted

One more Day,

One more week,

One more Month,

One more year.

Your wings were ready,

Long before our hearts

were ready to say good-bye,

Your wings were ready

It's your time to fly,

We all have to find our own way

To finally say Good-bye.

It's going to be hard

But it has to be done.

Your wings were ready

But our hearts were not....

<u>We're Watching Over You</u>

We're watching over You

The way we Did

On the day You Were Born.

So Small,

So Fragile.

We Loved You from The Very Start.

As you Grew

From Baby to Youth

And Youth to the Beautiful Woman

People Know you as Today.

We've Never Stopped Watching,

We've Been There Since the Beginning

And There 'til the end.

Even Though We have gone

To The Clouds Above,

We're Still Watching over You

The Way We Did

When You Were First Born,

Waiting to Hold you in our Arms Again.

Daddies LiL Girls

Some Things Change

And Some Remain

The Same Forever!

Daddies Lil Girls are what

We Will Always Be!

Sisters Together In Heaven

Forever Not Alone.

We will All Be Together

In the end.

Until that day,

We have each other.

You Will Forever

Be Our Daddy,

Forever We will Be

Daddies Lil Girls.

Some Things Change

And Some Remain

The Same Forever!

You Are our Daddy,

We Are Your Lil Girls.

Forever!

WE Love you Daddy!!

This Isn't Good-Bye

This isn't Goodbye,

Please Don't Cry.

I have Not left you, I am Not gone.

You can not see me, But I can still see you.

I will be there always,

Forever by your side.

Always Remember the Good Times.

The Love, The Laughs

We All shared.

This isn't Good-Bye,

Please Don't Cry.

I Have Not left, I am still Here.

Never too Far away,

One Day

You'll Be Back in my arms

Never to part again.

Please Don't Cry,

Because This Isn't Good-Bye.

I Have Not left you, I am still Here.

Watching over you,

Loving you

Like I was The Day you were Born.

So Please Don't Cry,

Because This Isn't Good-Bye.

Love Mom.

Thank-You from Above

A Thank-You from the heavens

Is what this is.

I'm sending down my Love

From up above.

You have always been there,

You have always cared.

When I got weak,

You Held my hand

And made me feel Strong.

I Wish I could have stayed,

I Wish I could be There.

Tell My Girls I miss Them,

Tell Them I am Still There

Watching over Them from above.

Tell Them I'll Always Love Them.

There's Not a Day that Goes By

Where I Don't Send down My Love.

Thank-You for being their Candle

When They Are Lost in the Dark.

Thank-You for being their Rock

When They are unable to find their own Strength.

A Thank-you from the Heavens

Is what this is.

I'm Sending Down My Love

From Up Above.

<u>One Long Drive</u>

One Long drive

To possibly say Goodbye,

To a Man I have Loved

Since the day I Was Born.

One Long Drive

To Possibly say Goodbye,

To a Man Who Has Loved Me

Since The day I was Born.

A Man Who watched Me Grow,

Who Taught Me Everything I know.

One Long Drive

To Possibly Say Goodbye,

To the only Father I'll Ever Have.

One Long Drive To wish, To Pray

That Everything Will Be OK.

One Long Drive To Cry, To Laugh

About All the Good Times Shared.

One Long Drive

To Possibly Say Goodbye Dad....

Born with Wings

I was born with wings,

It was my time To fly.

Long before

I learned how to walk.

Daddy,

Please don't be sad.

Mommy,

Please don't cry. You gave birth to an angle.

It was my time

To fly.

I have loved you both

Since the first beat of my heart.

Just like I know

I have been loved

Since the beginning.

I'll watch over you both

And wait till we are together again.

Daddy,

please don't be sad.

Mommy,

Please don't cry.

You gave birth to an angle

It was my time to fly.

Your Buddy

I Once Had

A Four Legged Mommy

Who Brought Me In To This World.

Than One Day

You Came In To My Life.

Now I Have A Two Legged Mommy.

13 Years Have Come And Gone.

All The Memories Will

Live On Forever In My Heart.

The Days Have Become long

And The Nights Longer.

Mommy Please Don't Cry,

I Don't Want To See You Sad.

There's A Place Called Heaven Mommy,

Where I will See You Again.

You've Given Me More Love

Than A Dog Could Ever Ask For.

Thank-You for

All The Treats,

All The Snuggles,

All The Love.

Thank-You For Everything,

This Is Not Good-Bye.

There's A Place Called Heaven Mommy,

Where I'll See You Again.

Where We Can Stay Together,

Forever!

You Will Always Be My Mommy

And I'll Always Be Your Buddy!

HEARTACHE

Everyone has experienced the feeling of having your heart torn out and trampled on, In Some way or the other. In this chapter, you will find poems about the pain and agony that is often associated with Heartaches. For those lucky people who have yet to experience the feeling of HEARTACHE, I hope you never have to feel that pain you will feel when a loved one rips your heart out with their palm of their hands. Its life, you never know who you can trust. These days most often it is the ones that you think you trust the most that turn out to be the ones that stab you in the back. Life is Crazy and this is just another Emotion we get to experience during our life time. Heartache is a result of trusting and loving the wrong people. If we Never let them in in the first place, We wouldn't be Butt-Hurt When shit hits the fan. At The same time, If we didn't let them in we wouldn't have been able to see their true colours. Lessons are learnt where you least expect it. People come and go through-out your life span, There's a Lesson to be learnt with everyone. At the end of the day; Always Trust your Heart!

Missing You

When I awake in the morning,

You are the first thing I think of.

Throughout the day

You're always on my mind.

I keep you close to my heart,

'cuz I love you.

I know you're far away But....

With me you'll always stay.

I miss you more than words can say.

I'm awaiting the day,

Till I can see you again.

At night when I fall asleep,

You're the last thought through my mind.

How I miss you so.

Why did you have to go,

And leave me like that.

We could have had it all

But that bullet to your head

Killed my dreams too.

A Broken Heart

I feel as though I lost a part of me.

A part that I need the most.

The other part of my heart.

I search for it everywhere

But yet never finding it.

I know someone must have it.

It must be the one who I thought

Would spend the rest of my life with me?

I call them on the phone, to my surprise

She is Home!

I ask her to tell me that she still loves me

But.........

She doesn't know.

I tell her that I love her

And ask her why the change!

She said people change And hangs up.

The dial tone kicks in.....

As I listen to it, I cry myself to sleep.

Wishing the dial tone would stop ringing in my Head!

<u>Why?</u>

Why do I Stay?

Why don't I Leave?

Why do I Love you?

Why don't I Hate you?

Why do I Cry?

Why don't I Laugh?

Why do I Stay?

Why don't I Leave?

Why...?

I Don't know!

Leavin'

I thought I knew you,

You thought you knew me.

This is why we can't be.

You knock me down And kick me around.

You're not the One for Me.

This is the way it's got to be.

You slap, you punch

And sometimes you almost kill.

I need to live my life Before it's too late.

Leaving you, Is the best thing I can do.

Its time for me to realize

You're never going to be the one

Who will be there forever.

Its better we move on now.

Save the tears, and the years.

The answer to the problem is

Leavin'!

and

I'm gone!

Heartache

Pain, so much pain!

Deep within this heart of mine.

I love this person

So much, it hurts.

Can't eat, can't sleep

But I can love. I can love so much.

This person is like an angel,

I dream about us being together.

Thinking it won't come true
Causes so much heartache.

So now I cry myself to sleep.

Wishing I could hold you tight.

Hoping this angel of mine

Really knows how I feel.

Hoping to see them in my dreams.

I cling to your photograph

And the memories we once shared.

It gets me through some nights,

When I can't have you here.

Tears

I watched you walk away,

My eyes filled with tears.

For every tear that fell, Had a Happy meaning to it.

Some were for kisses shared,

Others were for I love you's said.

As tears flow on and on

I smile remembering the good times.

I can't wait to have you in my arms once again

So we can make more memorable times.

With this tear, I quietly say I love you.

I fall asleep fast only to dream of you.

I awake in the morning

And realize that you're really gone!

The tears flow on and on.

Wish you were here and not there.

In my arms and not his!

<u>Everything</u>

If I told you everything my heart had to say

You'd come back

But I want you to come back on your own.

If you could see all my tears,

You'd run back just to hold me

But I want you to come back because you want too.

If you could read my mind You would see that I love you

But you'll learn soon enough.

You'll soon realize

That everything I have been saying is true.

I want you in my life to hold and most important to love.

I want it all down to the last drop.

You're the best thing that happened to me.

If I told you everything my heart has to say,

You'd come back

But I want you to come back on your own.

<u>Listen</u>

Listen!

Do you Hear that?

I do!

It's a cry from a girl with a Broken Heart.

She cries in agony!

Her tears flow with no life or meaning!

Look!

Do you see that?

I do!

The pain she's going through

I caused that broken heart

What can I do, I caused all this!

Man oh mam, am I ever a prick!

I can't sleep, I hear her crying!

I feel her pain; it's driving me insane!

Listen!

Do you hear that?

I do!

Piece it Back Together

Listening to a song, Brings you to mind.

I miss your soft skin, Your sweet kisses.

I wish I could go back in time,

To a time when you were in

My arms, but that can't be.

A love like ours can't be.

For you are the one who

Ripped my heart from my chest

With those dirty hands of yours.

Sometimes I miss you, But other times I hate you

For thinking I was no good.

I still carry your picture with me

Don't know why, but I still do.

Hopefully one day I will piece back together

That heart you thought was a toy;

When you took it from me, and walked all over it.

I hope you feel good

But one day I will piece it back together

And be able to love again.

Left Behind

You turned the page

And left me behind.

I thought we'd be forever

But now were on two different pages.

I wish I only knew

What to say or do

To get back into your arms.

Things happen for a reason

Maybe this is where we are supposed to be

But my heart thinks different.

I thought we'd be forever

But you turned the page

and left me Behind.

Goodbye

I watch you walk away

Knowing you'll never return

Back to my home, Back to my heart.

It hurts so much to let you go.

I want to run to you, hold you

And tell you I love you.

This is for the better.

As you get on the bus,

You turn my way, and say Goodbye.

I say goodbye and then turn away.

I miss you now, like I missed you then.

Will you ever come back home?

I hope so, but you said goodbye.

Not see you in the future.

So I know you will never

Step through my door again.

I missed you now like I miss you then.

So now I say goodbye to the love we once had.

And try to let you go.

Before you Go

Before you walk away,

Look into my eyes

and see what my heart is trying to say.

It cries out for you to love it back.

Look into my soul

and see what its trying to say.

It yearns to be held by you.

I don't think I could go on,

If you are not in my life.

I need you

Like the night needs the stars.

So before you go,

Look into my eyes.

There you'll see the love I have for you.

And maybe you'll stay.

Maybe!

No turning Back

I once saw a future

And had lots of hope.

Now I see darkness And left feeling empty.

Life has changed

Through your eyes and mine.

It was so nice and peaceful

And love was in the air.

What went wrong?

Our love was so strong!

How could we let it

Crash and burn.

Dreams forever changed,

Dreams that will never be.

We once loved

But now we lost.

There's no turning back!

What was, is No more.

It's gone forever...

There's No turning Back!

By a Different Name

Last night While we laid in bed.

You called me

By a different name.

I wanted to scream and shout

But instead I bit my Tongue.

For another fight I did not want.

As we lay there in the dark

No works were spoken.

You drifted off to sleep

As I lay there thinking.

That night While we laid in bed.

You called me

By a different name.

I wanted to scream and shout

But instead I bit my tongue

And said nothing.

Played

You played me for a fool,

I can clearly see that now.

I wasn't the only boy, You had hanging around.

I gave you my heart, Thinking that you'd be true.

It broke in half

When I saw him holding you.

You played me for a fool

And broke this heart of mine.

I wonder how many times

You've committed this crime

Or how many hearts you've broken along the way.

You played me for a fool.

Oh how I wish I wasn't one of those fools

That played your game And lost their mind.

Maybe next time,

I wont be so Blind!

Pain like No Other

I try to hide the tears,

I try to hide the pain

But nothing seems to work

When my hearts broken in 2.

It hurts so much

To keep it all inside.

Sometimes I wish I'd just die,

Just so you wouldn't see me cry.

I try to run,

I try to hide!

No matter where I go

Or what I do,

Heartache always finds its way back to me.

It's too much to take at times.

I try to sleep

But it finds me in my dreams.

Its everywhere I go.

I just want to be happy,

Is that to much to ask?

I try to hide the tears,

I try to hide the pain,

When heartache comes knocking...

It will find a way in...

Dark-side!

I would like to believe that everyone has a Dark side, which we are just born within us. I have a dark side, it's a lot darker than most as you will soon realize... I also Believe that most people hide from their dark side in fear of what they might find. In this chapter, There's no Hiding anything. I dug and dug and dug some more until I got to the bottom of the madness. These poems are out there and they say everything and leaves nothing to the imagination. You're about to enter the Darkest part of the Book! These poems have the Darkest of feelings, pain and sadness. They are Dark and Scary but they needed to be in here because I know that there are millions of people around the world who have felt this way before or are feeling this way now. I just want to say to them that there are many ways you can take your feelings out; I chose poetry to get those feelings out, so that they are not kept inside. These poems were created with events in either my own or the lives of people that are close to me. I really hope you enjoy your ride on the DARK SIDE!

Sad World

The World Is A Beautiful Place,

If You Can Look past The BullShit.

If You Look Closer,

You'll Soon Realize

The Sad World

We All Live In.

You Get More Time

For Selling A Bag Of Weed On The Streets

Than A Man Who Touches

Little Boys In The Sheets.

People Killing People

Because The Colour Of Their Skin

Or Who they Choose To Love.

Too Many People

Sleeping On The Streets

Without Enough Food To Eat.

Our Children Are No Longer Safe,

It's a Sad World We Live In.

It's a Sad Place,

We Have Made For Ourselves!

The World Is A Beautiful Place,

If You Can Look Past The BullShit.

Monster in the Closet

Frightened & Scared,

Alone with You.

You Shouldn't Be Here

Who Let You In...

One Night Over 20 Years Ago

Has Changed My Life Forever.

I still Feel Your Dirty Hands,

Still Hear Your Voice.

Monster in the Closet,

Will You Ever Leave And Leave Me Be?

You Should Not Have Been Here,

Who Let You in.

The Answer Still Echoes in my Head.

" Little One Don't Fear, Your Mother Let Me in"

Frightened & Scared

Alone with You.

You Shouldn't Be Here,

Who Let You in

" Your Mommy Did"!

<u>Who should I Blame</u>

Who Should I Blame,

You or Him?

Who Should I Hate,

You or Him?

Who Should I forgive,

You or Him?

These Are Questions

That Run Through My Mind.

The Answers Never Change.

I Blame You Both.

I'll Hate You Both.

For as Long as I Live,

No Matter How Hard I try

I'll Never Be able to Forgive you

Both......

No Matter How High I get,

I can Never Manage to Forget

The Blame, The Rage, The Hate

I Feel When Either of you come to mind.

On this Day

On This Day

I should be out shopping,

Looking for the Perfect card

And picking out Pretty Flowers.

On This Day

I should be at home,

Baking The Perfect Birthday Cake

And putting a Pretty bow on a box.

On This Day

I should be packing up my car,

Driving hours to come see you.

On this Day

I should be Happy; I should be Cheerful

But I'm Not......

Only Thing I'm Doing

Is Wishing you'd Die...

I Hate You

I Hate you now, Like a hated you then.

I'm a changed man

You're still the mom, I never wanted.

You were never there; never really cared.

Now that it's said and done with,

I'm glad you weren't there.

You've missed so much in my life; my son's life;

I have not missed a thing.

I'll grow up and move on,

I miss you now Like I missed you then.

You were never the Mom I needed.

You'll never have the chance to fuck up at being a grandmother.

One day you'll see,

That all of this didn't have to be.

You could have been there,

You could have cared!

I'll hate you always,

like I hate you now!

Four cuts I'm out

As I sit down on my bed, I think of my shitty life,

Wishing I could do something about

the way people look at me.

I begin to cut my arm,

for all the stuff that has gone wrong.

The first cut is for the people

who made me feel I was good for nothing.

The second is for the hurt I am going though.

The third is for not believing in me

when I said I could do it.

The last Cut is for all the people who said

they could do better without me.

I fall to the floor, knowing I am going to face death.

Thinking to myself, maybe now people can be happy.

I fall into my endless sleep of happiness.

Overlooking my Dead body,

I soon Realize the mistake that I've made.

I am Not Happier; I am Not free.

I am gone!

This wasn't God's plan for me.

Boy, did I ever mess up

what was meant to be.

I am not happier; I am not free.

I am just gone!

Orphan

I only Feel like an orphan

On the Days

I think of you.

I Don't Recall

A Touch from a Mother

Or the Love

From a Father.

Those Feelings

Have long Vanished.

I Don't Remember

What it's like

To Be Someone's Son

Or Part of their Family.

I don't Remember Your Voice

Or

Your Gentle Touch.

I only feel like an Orphan

On the days I think of you.

So I try my best not 2.

What can I Say

What can I say, To a person like you?

Other than, I Hate you!

I still can't believe,

I wasted all my time on something like you.

I should have realized sooner

and left your crazy-ass behind.

It's true what they say,

You learn from your mistakes,

You were a big Mistake.

I've learned my lesson

On loving people

Who only love themselves?

So what can I say, To a person like you?

Other than,

I Hate you!

Daddy, oh daddy

Daddy, oh daddy

I wish I could tell you,

That I'm in a better place now.

I can't because I'm lonely.

There's no one here to talk to,

No one to lean on when I'm sad.

When I'm happy, I have no one to laugh with.

I'm not sure where I am; I think its hell.

I wish I was home but I'm gone, gone from you for good.

I just want you to know,

That it was me who picked up that razor.

I'm sorry you had to be the one to find me,

Lying on the bathroom floor.

Sorry for all the mess I made,

Blood all over the floor.

I always thought it would be better,

If I was out of everybody's life.

After all of this, I guess I was wrong.

I feel bad for all the hurt you are going through.

I wish I could give you a hug, and tell you I'm sorry.

Daddy, oh daddy

Please understand,

That I still love you,

And...

I'm really sorry!

Thoughts of Suicide

Thoughts of you Fill my troubled head.

I want to love you

But you're nowhere to be found.

I look and look

But still I can't find your love.

I miss your love so much, that it just kills me.

The thought of suicide enters my head.

I try to push it out

But I can't, it wants to stay.

So I think it over,

With every passing minute

It starts to sound better, and better.

As time passes,

I decide

That it's the only way.

I run to the bathroom

Grab the razor and start to cut.

I do it once, twice

Until my arm looks like an endless railroad.

I begin to get dizzy and fall to the floor.

My last thoughts are of you.

I just hope you know that

You were my true love

And that it was the...

Thoughts of suicide.

<u>......But then came You</u>

I remember,

A time when I could love.

When I knew how I felt

About love, about life.

A time when love was in my eyes

And music in my soul.

But then came you.

You took the love from my eyes

And the music from my soul.

At night I'd cry myself to sleep,

Hoping you'd stop

But... You didn't, you just kept on.

Turning my happy life into

A dark and cold nightmare.

You took my heart and

Threw it out a window.

It fell down, down Into a Great dark sea of pain.

My life was great

But... Then came you!

The Pill

I once vision your first cry

But it was muted because

The pill!

I once vision holding you

But you slipped through my hands because

The pill!

I once vision your first step

But you fell before you stood because

The pill!

I once vision your first Birthday

But you never grew that old because

The pill!

I once vision your first day of school

But you couldn't go because

The pill!

I once vision your birth

But your death came first because....... The pill!

Player

You played with my heart.

You thought it was a toy!

What the fuck were you trying to see?

How many times it would fucking break!

I caught on to your game too soon

So you only got a chance to break it once.

I loved you once, But NEVER again!

I can't believe I cried over you

and wasted all those tears!

For you would never shed a tear for anyone.

I'm happy to say that I got over you

By getting under someone new.

The only thing is I'm kicking myself

For ever going out with a whore like you

But I have lived and learned.

I'll never forget

That you're a mind playing

Heartbreaking

Fucking Slut!

Suicide is too Close

Thinking of suicide makes me sick

But yet it's always in the back of my head.

Suicide is not painful; at least that's what I read.

Sitting in my room

Thinking if I should end it all, but how?

I think to myself that death does not scare me now.

I'm so sick of all this shit.

Wishing I was in a hole, left to die.

No one loves me! No one is there!

What am I here for? There's got to be a place for me

Its just not here!

Suicide is too close.

Empty pill bottle on the floor,

There's got to be a place for me,

Where I can be free!

Eyes closed, Heart stopped, Gone forever!

'Cause you're too Late

If I am Gone, Before You Wake.

Don't Go Looking, 'Cause You're Too Late.

You'll Find Me where you least Expect.

Don't Go in Your Closet

And Push Your Clothes Aside.

'Cause You just might Find Me; Hanging Inside.

I Tried to Hide it, I Tried to Fight it.

All the Feeling I kept inside

It Became to Strong.

There was No Other Way,

It Had to Be Done.

The Rope Was Tight,

The White Light was Bright.

I Hope You Miss Me,

I Hope You Cry at Night.

You Made Me Do This,

With All Your Lies.

So If I am Gone, Before You Wake.

Don't Go Looking, 'Cause You're Too Late.

Little Voices

Little voices in my head,

Tell me that I should be dead.

To live with you

Is worse than being dead.

You bring me down,

I can't seem to rise.

You kick me when I am up,

Push me when I am down.

Little voices in my head

Tell me to leave you,

That you're not the one for me.

I don't know you,

You don't know me.

Yet we thought we could be.

It's gone on to long,

My heart can't stand the pain.

Little voices in my head,

Tell me it would be better if I were dead.

Away from you, away from the pain.

Miscellaneous

This is the Last chapter to your Poetic Journey with me. I can't believe it!!! I Hate to see it end... I Hope you have enjoyed the ride with me. I had to put these poems in the book but didn't really know where to put some of them, so heres to the Last Chapter! In this chapter you will find a little bit of everything rolled into one. Enjoy!!!! I Just want to thank you again and again for picking this Book up and Entering my CRAZY World. It has Been in the works for many years and I am Completely Thrilled to have it Finally Completed. I Hope that you have Enjoyed the Book. Thanks Again from the Bottom of my Heart! A Lot of Sweat and Tears have gone into making this Creation. Much LOVE to EVERYONE READING THIS RIGHT Meow.

<u>Beautiful Disaster</u>

A Beautiful Disaster

Is What I am.

A Man Loved A Woman

And A Beautiful Disaster

Was Born.

Like fire to the rain

Their love was gone

But I still remain.

Split Between homes,

Split Between Parents.

Back and Forth, Back and Forth.

A Beautiful Disaster

Is What I am.

Here because

A Woman loved

A Man.......

Just Look

When I look into your eyes

They tell me everything.

If I ever wonder how you feel,

I just look into your eyes

And find the truth behind the lies.

I find your true feelings,

I see all your hopes & dreams.

Shinning like a bright star.

You've captured my heart

With just one look.

How I love to look into your eyes

To see your true beauty.

So whenever I need answers

I just look into your eyes.

They tell me everything I need to know....

Falling in Love

Falling in love is good,

When it's with the right person.

It ends in a broken heart

When it's with the wrong person.

As for me, I have found that right person.

He's the type to kiss the ground I walk on.

He's there to catch me,

if ever I fall.

He is my life,

The one who won my heart

By taking me by the hand

And making me feel like

I am his

whole world....

<u>Untitled</u>

When I see you in the hall,

My heart stops for a second

And the world seems still.

For that one second

My heart fills with joy,

Knowing that I'm falling in love all over again.

When I come back to reality, you are gone.

I want to run and find you.

I wish I could tell you how I feel.

Not knowing if I should or shouldn't.

I know I love you but I don't even know how you feel.

I wish I could hold you for a lifetime

But now it's only in my dreams.

Maybe one day we'll be together

And it could be real.

I Wish

I wish for your love,

To be back in my life; Day and night.

I miss you more and more

With each passing day.

I just want to be The one you need

When you are sad.

The one to listen,

When you have a joke to tell.

I wish I could tell you I dream of a beach,

Walking barefoot in the sand you and I.

The water brushes our feet

With you holding my hand and my heart at the same time.

I wish You knew how I need your hugs & kisses

To brighten my days

And your soft lips and your tender embrace

To warm up those lonely nights.

I wish You were here right now

Holding me close.

I wish, Oh How I wish.

<u>Love</u>

Love

Is more than

Just a feeling!

Love can make

Or break

Your heart!

Love can grow into a beautiful rose

Or shatter like a stained-glass window.

Love can put a smile on your face

Or tears in your eyes.

Love is a powerful thing,

So think twice before playing that game.

It could be great

Or it could ruin you...

I See

I see your tears,

Although you don't show them.

I see your pain,

Although you don't know it.

I see the beauty in you,

When you see nothing.

I see the love in your heart,

When you find nothing but an empty space.

But what I can't see is,

Why can't you see me?

Why don't you see how I feel?

See that I love you

And that you are my world

I see you.

Why?

Why don't you

See me?

I Hope

Dear friend,

Please stop running, for your feet must be tired.

Give me your hand, for I'll never hurt you.

I've tried to open your eyes to let you see the real world,

But for some reason you run.

Why...? What has happened to you?

Your feet must be so sore, please stop running!

Take a seat and rest awhile, Talk to me about your hurt.

Don't be afraid, for I'll never break your heart.

Listen to the beat of my heart, then you'll know

My love is true.

We are the best of friends and closer at times

Until you started running again!

Please stop running, and sit and talk with me.

I miss you,

I'm afraid that you Have ran to far out of my reach.

I hope you'll come back one day, One day soon!

Maybe stay awhile, take off those running shoes and enjoy

The sand between your toes...

How I Feel

Dear friend, I wish I could tell you

How I feel; I'm scared, so scared

Of what you might say.

I want to be with you

Until the end of time.

Till the sun no longer shines,

Till the last star shoots across the sky.

You showed me the real world

And took me on a wicked ride.

Your friendship is very important to me.

If I ever lost it, I would go insane.

You might not know this, but

The is coming from the bottom of

My broken heart.

You mean the world to me

And just thought you ought to know.

Angel

Kissed by an angel

Is what it feels like.

When your lips touch mine.

Touched by an angel

Is what it feels like.

When your hands touch mine.

Held by an angel

Is what it feels like.

When you hold me in your arms.

You're my angel!

My love, My safe ground, My best friend!

No one can take your place,

it doesn't get better than you.

You are my man!

You are my Today,

My Tomorrow,

My forever!

J'Taime

Hands

When I put these hands to work,

They can do marvelous things.

When it seems the world is on your back

Ill pick you up and help you back to your feet.

When it seems the world has let you down

Ill lift you up so you can touch the sky.

When it seems the world has turned its back on you,

I will hold you close and keep you safe.

My hands are nothing special,

They are the same as the man besides me

But what is different is the love I have for you.

When I put these hands to work,

They can do marvelous things.

They will pick you up when you are down.

Hold you close and keep you warm

But most of all These hands will hold your heart

And make sure it doesn't break.

I'll hold it now; I'll hold it for a lifetime!

I'm Never letting go!

<u>You tell Me</u>

You tell me I'm in the wrong,

You tell me I'm the worst of all.

You tell me to let you Be,

You tell me

To just leave!

You tell me

What I can't give you.

You tell me

 You hate me

But than

You tell me

You love me!

And

I believe you

And I Stay......!

Picture of Us

The picture of us Is fading fast.

Where it was once clear and beautiful,

Is now dark and gloomy!

The plans that we once had

Were once achievable,

Now they seem unreachable.

I wanted to spend the rest of my life with you,

Now it's not the same.

I want to be gone

Away from this,

Away from the pain.

Loving you was the best

And the worst thing to do.

The picture of us is fading fast,

For the love is gone

Like a STAR that shines no more.

Even When

Even when we fight

And I'm filled with rage,

I still see forever

When looking into your Beautiful eyes!

Even when we don't speak

And the I love you's aren't said,

I still know deep down you care.

Even when we don't touch

I wait till you fall asleep

Just to hold you in my arms.

Even when we fight

And I'm filled with rage

I still see Forever

When looking into your Beautiful eyes.

Every Time

Every time

You think the pieces fit,

They are always falling apart!

Every time

You think you see me smiling,

I am always crying on the inside.

Every time

You and I go for walks,

We always walk alone.

Every time

Things seems perfect,

Their NOT!

EVERY TIME!

Would You

If I gave you the pieces

To this shattered heart of mine,

Would you be a friend

And make it whole again?

If a gave you all my tears

From this broken soul of mine,

Would you be a friend

And make my eyes dry again?

If I came to you

And confined in you,

Would you be a friend

And stick around till the end?

Dust in the Wind

Pen in hand,

Words on paper.

Feelings pouring out.

Filled with Anger,

Filled with Hate.

To much pain

Kept inside for to long.

Time to let go, To let go of all this!

All of this Hate, All of the Anger!

Pen in hand.

Words on paper.

Letting it all go!

No more pain,

No more tears!

Lighter in hand,

Flame to Paper!

Watching it all Burn.

Paper to Dust,

Dust to the wind!

<u>Come Rain or Shine</u>

Come Rain or Shine

I Got you on my Mind.

You're The only one I think about,

The only one I Dream about.

Come Rain or Shine

I Got you on my mind.

In the Morning

Or in the Evening,

I Got you on my mind.

I Love You,

Like No Other.

Come Rain or Shine,

There's One Thing you can count on;

I Got you on my mind....

White Picket Fence

Behind The White Picket fence

Is where true Love Blossoms.

Where the sun Always Shines.

Where the grass

Grows the Greenest.

Behind The White Picket fence

Is where We live,

Where we Laugh,

Where we Love.

The life I've Always Dreamed,

The Love I've Always Wanted,

Everything I'll Ever Need and More

Is all in You.

Behind The White Picket fence

Is where You & I call HOME.

True Love Lives and Grows There.

JUST Behind,

THE White Picket Fence.

In the Stars

It's written in the stars,

It's Clear to see.

A Love like ours

Is meant to be.

The Power,

The Sparks

When we Touch, When we Kiss.

You Would have to be Blind

If you Don't See,

A Love like ours

Is Meant to Be.

The Magic,

The Fireworks

When we Touch, When we Kiss.

It's Written in the STARS,

It's Clear to see

A LOVE like OURS

Is Meant to BE.

If

If I Die Before My time,

Just know I've Never Really Left.

I am Always by your side.

I'll be the drops in the rain,

The wind in the breeze.

I Love you more and more

As the Days Go On.

If I die Before My Time

Just know that I am Always There.

Just like the Leafs in the fall,

The snow in the Winter.

I Will Always be There.

So If I Die Before My Time,

Just Know I'll Always Love You

And You're Never Alone

Because I Never Really Left You...

Falling Teardrops

Falling Teardrops,

Never Ending pain.

Day After Day

The Pain Remains The Same.

Falling Teardrops,

Never Ending Nightmare.

Sleepless Nights,

Colds Sweats,

Broken Hearted.

Falling Teardrops,

Never Ending Pain.

Year After Year,

The Pain Remains

The Same.

Falling Teardrops

Day After Day....

Stop Looking Back

Stop Looking Back,

Leave The Past Behind you.

Leave The Pain, Leave The Hurt.

Stop Looking Back,

Keep Looking Forward.

Enjoy What is in Front of you.

Enjoy Your Today, and Tomorrow.

Stop Looking Back,

Leave The Past Behind You.

Yesterday Was SHIT,

Your Past Is way Behind you.

Stop Looking Back

And

Leave The Past Behind you.

Today Is Beautiful

So Stop Looking Back...

Forever

Forever...

Written in Ink

For Now, Until Eternity.

For The Whole World to See.

Forever,

Is How Long I Plan

On Loving you.

Forever

Is How Long I Gave you

My Heart For.

Forever,

Is Our Game Plan.

Forever You Are Mine,

Forever I am Yours.

Forever

Written in Ink

Etched in Our Hearts

Forever......

Burnt Bridges

Burnt Bridges,

I've Caused Many.

Most of Which

Have Been Forgotten.

People Come,

People Go.

Sometimes People Fuck Up

And Mistakes Are Made.

All Can Be Forgotten

Sometimes....

Burnt Bridges

I've Caused Many

Some Are Forgotten

And Some Are Worth

Rebuilding.........

How do I Say I'm Sorry

How Do You Say I'm Sorry?

When Those Words Have Lost All Meaning.

How Do You Say I'm Sorry?

When All I Can Do Is Fuck Everything Up.

I Want to Make It All Better,

I want to get Back

To where We Belong;

Where it All Began.

Where The Love Was Pure,

Where Time Stood Still,

Where it was Just you & I.

How Do you say, I'm Sorry?

When Those Words

Have Lost All Meaning.

You Don't,

You Shut your Mouth

And Prove my love to you.

Actions Speak Louder Than Words

So Let Me Prove my love to you.

Last Chance

Last Chances, I've Had Plenty.

I Don't Know why you stay,

Why Don't You Run.

Chance After Chance,

I Seem to Blow Them All.

I Shatter Everything I Touch

With These Broken Hands of Mine.

Last Chances, I've Had Plenty.

I Always Find a Way

To Fuck Everything up.

I Don't Know Why, I Just Can't Get It Right.

No Matter How Many Times I Fuck Up

I Always Pray You'll Give Me

One Last Chance.

Last Chances, I've Had Plenty.

Maybe This Time,

I can Get My Shit Together.

To Love You Right

Forever, As Planned.

YOU

You are Perfect,

Your Love is Magical;

Your There

Because you care.

There's No Doubt

Who You Love

Or Where You Should Be.

Not Only Are You Perfect,

You're Perfect for Me.

You Are Truth,

You're The Real Deal.

You're Amazing,

The Best Part About You

Is That You're

MINE!

Lights On

I Sleep with the Lights on

When You Are Not Home,

That way I don't feel alone.

In our bed

Without you,

The world Seems Big and Scary;

So I sleep with the Lights on

When you are not Home.

The Lights Go Off

When you come through that Door,

The World seems Perfect Again.

You Are My Light,

You are My World.

I Sleep with the lights on

When you are not Home,

So I feel less Alone.

Lost Kisses

Lost Kisses, Is what it is

When Time is Being Spent

Angry or Mad.

Lost Hugs, Is All It is

When Time is Being Spent

Accusing or Hurting.

The Times I've Spent

Treating you like Shit,

I could have Been

Kissing you, Loving you.

All The Times I spent

Accusing you

Of outlandish Things,

I Could have been

Holding you in my Arms.

All This Time I wasted

is Lost Kisses And Lost Hugs

No More Bullshit;

I Want the Kisses, I want The Hugs

<u>Blink of an Eye</u>

In a Blink of an eye,

This could all be Gone.

No More You, No More Me, No More Us.

In The Blink of an eye,

Our World Could Change; Forever.

Hold Me Tight, Love Me Right.

Make Me the one you need

In The middle of the Night.

This is Perfect,

This is Great.

I want this Forever

But

In a Blink of an eye

This could all be gone.

No More you, No More me, No More us.

So Hold Me Tight And

Love Me Right

'Cause in A Blink of an Eye

It Could All Be Gone.

Run

Why Do I run away from you?

You've always been There,

You've Always Cared.

You've Never Wanted to Run,

You've Never Wanted to Leave.

Through all my ups and downs,

You've Always stuck around.

You've Never Given up on us.

Why Do I run away from you?

You've Always Been There,

You've Always Cared.

You Love me for my Bad, You Love me for my Good.

You take me, Just the way I am.

You Never Wanted to Run,

You Never Wanted to Leave.

From Now on

I Need to Run to You,

Into your Loving Arms

That Want to Hold Me...

Not Like HER

I'm Not Like Her, In Anyway.

I Wouldn't Have

Done you Wrong,

Played You For a Fool!

I'm Not Like Her, In Anyway.

I Never Did

The Shit She Did.

I Don't Know Why

You Don't Trust Me?

I'm Not Like Her, In Anyway.

I Never Did You Wrong

Or Played You Along.

I'm Not Like Her, In Anyway

Other Than

WE Both Don't Have

You.......

I'm Done

I'm Done

Believing in Love.

Thinking There's a

You & Me.

I'm Done

Thinking We're

On The Same Page.

I'm Done

Thinking There's a Future.

That Day is Always So Far Away.

I'm Done

Thinking you Trust Me

Because If You Did

Your Comments

Wouldn't Be Made.

I'm Done

Believing in Love,

I'm Done

Believing in Us.

Final Thoughts

Well it looks like you finished the Book. I really hope you enjoyed your Journey through all the emotions this books has to offer. I will never be able to thank you enough for taking the time to pick up this Book and giving it a shot. Thank you for letting me be a part of your own Journey in life. This book has been in the works for a really really really long time now, I am Sooo pleased with how it All came together and turned out. I hope copies of this book still make it around this crazy place Long after I am gone. I'm still in shock that the book is finally finished, That I finally finished it!! I Honestly felt like it would never get done But it did. Your living proof of that, you're holding the book in your hands right now. Within this book is my heart and soul over all the pages! So many tears, Both the good and the bad have gone into Writing, Revising and finally completing this Book! 100% Raw emotions Run through each page of this Book. If you take Anything away from reading this Book let it include the following to always remember and live by:

1. Life is Short, Make The Most Out of IT!

2. Love with NO Regrets!

3. There is Still Good in This World!

4. You are the ONLY YOU, that will ever Be! You are Perfect, You are Beautiful!

5. Live Laugh Love

Life is hard Enough without the added Bullshit of Everything else. Stay positive! Keep your head held High! Don't EVER let someone tell you that you're not worth it!!! When life gets hard and you don't think you can go on another day, Remember you're not alone. Life gets Really Tough Sometimes But if We Give Up and throw in the towel; you'll Never Be able to Fully Enjoy Everything this Crazy Life has to offer... Don't Frown, Cause you'll Never know who's Falling for Your Smile!! Let The World See Your Beautiful Eyes and Smile. Life is Shit Sometimes There's No Sugar Coating that one!! Sometimes it Fucking Sucks!! Don't Let it get you Down! You are STRONG, You Got THIS!! Never Give Up!! You will Never know HOW FAR YOU can GO, if you STOP Now! Don't Give up, Don't Look Back!! Keep Moving Forward! You Get ONE LIFE, LIVE it UP!! Yesterday, Today, Tomorrow Be the Best version of Yourself That You Can Be!! When Life Gets Hard, Stare at it in the face and Tell it to FUCKING Suck IT! You Are Better than THAT!! You Will Not Give Up!! You Will Show YourSelf and Everyone Else just what you're Made of!! Don't EVER Forget to Love YourSelf First.

In closing;

Be The Change you want to See in The World!!!

Live Laugh Love!

Thank you so much ONE Last Time,
Love Always,

Jason Buckley

Lightning Source UK Ltd.
Milton Keynes UK
UKHW010753081119
353112UK00001B/19/P